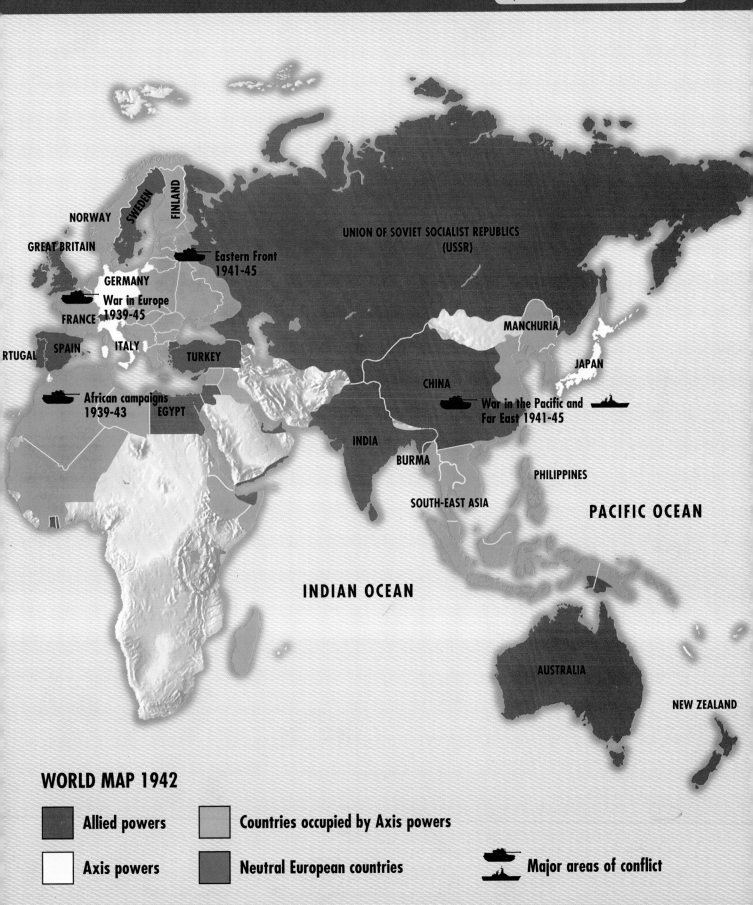

NORWAY

SWEDEN

FINLAND

GREAT BRITAIN

UNION OF SOVIET SOCIALIST REPUBLICS
(USSR)

Eastern Front
1941-45

GERMANY

War in Europe
1939-45

FRANCE

MANCHURIA

RTUGAL

SPAIN

ITALY

JAPAN

TURKEY

CHINA

African campaigns
1939-43

EGYPT

War in the Pacific and
Far East 1941-45

INDIA

BURMA

PHILIPPINES

SOUTH-EAST ASIA

PACIFIC OCEAN

INDIAN OCEAN

AUSTRALIA

NEW ZEALAND

WORLD MAP 1942

Allied powers

Countries occupied by Axis powers

Axis powers

Neutral European countries

Major areas of conflict

THE ROAD TO WAR
1919-1939

The First World War started in 1914, almost by accident. In 1919 the Treaty of Versailles was meant to ensure there would be no more wars. Yet the Second World War started in 1939 as its tragic and inevitable consequence.

The signing of the Treaty of Versailles in 1919 – a painting by British artist Sir William Orpen.

The Treaty of Versailles, 1919

The Treaty was the work of the three victorious leaders, Georges Clemenceau of France, Woodrow Wilson of the USA and David Lloyd George of Great Britain. It set up the League of Nations to stop future conflicts. It also accused Germany of all war-guilt, imposed huge reparations (fines) and forbade it to re-arm. Germany must never be a threat again.

The Treaty was a disaster. The League of Nations was nothing but a talking shop. The treatment of Germany caused it dishonour and disgrace; but no proud people will put up with such humiliation for long. The German army had never actually been defeated in the war.

Germans believed the old guard – the Kaiser (king) and the politicians – had let their soldiers down. Simmering resentment and discontent were bound to boil over.

Adolf Hitler

By 1929 the world was in economic chaos with unemployment, strikes and social unrest – and nowhere more so than Germany. Extremism spread – fascism and communism seemed to offer ways out of the mess.

Adolf Hitler had been a corporal in the German army. Disgusted with the 1918 Armistice, he became lader of his National Socialist (Nazi) Party, preaching German nationalism, racism, strong leadership and

> "The aim of German policy is to make sure to preserve the racial community and to enlarge it. It is therefore a question of *Lebensraum* (living space)."
>
> Adolf Hitler, 5 November 1937

revenge. In the 1920s Germany was in chaos; revolution was inevitable and in 1933 it came. Hitler was appointed chancellor and made himself a dictator – the *Führer* (leader). He began to re-arm Germany and to plan for a new world order based on Aryan or Germanic "racial purity" and German mastery. This Third Reich (empire) would, he said, last for a thousand years. But first, he had to make Germany invincible in war.

Adolf Hitler takes the salute at the Nazi Party's Nuremberg Rally of 1934.

The Allied Powers

After 1919, the world was sick of war. There were other things to think about. In Britain, labour unrest culminated in the 1926 General Strike. In the United States there was the great economic crash in the stock market in 1929, resulting in industries going bankrupt overnight. The effects of this spread from the USA all over the world. In Russia, the communist revolution was complete. In Italy, Benito Mussolini's Fascist Party came to power. Another war was the last thing Europe wanted.

While Germany re-armed, other countries were reducing their fighting forces. Even when people recognised the threat posed by Hitler, the policy of many governments was to avoid war at all costs.

Expansion

Hitler wanted more than an alliance of German-speaking peoples: he wanted a unified country. In 1938, his troops marched unopposed into Austria. The first part of his expansion eastwards was successful.

The Sudetenland, in western Czechoslovakia, had been German before the Treaty of Versailles. Hitler wanted it back to accommodate an expanding Aryan race.

To Neville Chamberlain, prime minister of Britain, Czechoslovakia was "a far-away country of which we know little", not worth risking war for. He flew to Hitler's summer home, Berchtesgaden, and on 30 September 1938 signed the fateful Munich Agreement. Hitler could do as he liked in the east. Chamberlain thought he had "peace with honour" and Britain breathed a sigh of relief.

"I believe it (the Munich Agreement) is peace for our time."

Neville Chamberlain, 30 September 1938

Poland

So who was next? Former German territories such as Upper Silesia and Danzig were now part of Poland: Germany wanted them too. Besides, Poles weren't Aryan. To Nazis, Slavs were *Untermenschen* (inferior people). After taking Czechoslovakia, Hitler signed a pact with Soviet leader Joseph Stalin to help each other in war and divide Poland between them. On 1 September 1939 Germany invaded.

Polish forces were brave but their equipment was obsolete: Hitler practised the *Blitzkrieg* (lightning war) tactics he would use in France. The *Wehrmacht* (German army) was ruthless and ordinary people were as much targets as soldiers. Germany over-ran western Poland, while Russia invaded from the east.

German troops attack Poland in September 1939.

> **Not even Chamberlain could let this go. Holland, Belgium, Denmark and France would be next, then perhaps Britain itself.**

On 3 September 1939 Britain declared war on Nazi Germany. France declared on the same day. The British Empire – countries such as Canada, Australia and New Zealand – followed.

For six months nothing happened: a time that quickly became known as the "Phoney War". London's air-raid warnings sounded, but no bomber aeroplanes came. It was as if the opposing powers did not want to provoke each other.

Winston Churchill addresses sailors in London in April 1940, just before becoming prime minister.

Denmark and Norway

On 9 April 1940 war became a reality when Hitler invaded both Denmark and Norway. To save lives, the Danish army was ordered not to fight and the government called a ceasefire.

The Germans had believed they could take Norway without a fight if the Nazi sympathiser Vidkun Quisling formed a government. But Norway rejected him, so Hitler struck. Allied forces sent to defend Norway now saw what manner of opponent Germany was. Soon the British and French withdrew, to prepare for the bigger battle to come.

Winston Churchill

In Britain, one of the most important acts of the war now took place. In April, before Germany invaded Norway, Neville Chamberlain announced that Hitler had "missed the bus". Now Parliament turned against him. Under pressure, Chamberlain resigned and Winston Churchill became prime minister.

> "You have sat too long here for any good you have been doing. Depart, I say, and let us have done with you. In the name of God, go!"
>
> These words by Oliver Cromwell were quoted to Neville Chamberlain, 7 May 1940

Hitler poses proudly in front of the Eiffel Tower after the fall of France in June 1940.

Hitler now accomplished in six weeks what Germany failed to do in four years during the First World War: conquer France.

The French had been seared by the events of 1914-18. They had believed in *élan* (constant attack), but only grim defence saved them. In the 1930s they had built the Maginot Line – a chain of modern concrete forts – which stretched from the south of France to the Belgian border. They had intended this to be an impregnable barrier to an invader. But it failed to stop the destructive power of the Wehrmacht.

More countries fall

On 10 May, the day Churchill became prime minister of Britain, the Wehrmacht invaded the Netherlands, Belgium and Luxembourg. The small Dutch and Belgian armies were over-run. Luxembourg had no army.

German troops entered France from the north, also on 10 May. The main thrust, spearheaded by German *Panzer* (tank) divisions, was through the wooded, mountainous Ardennes region, which the French believed to be impenetrable. While some German troops kept the Maginot Line busy, others burst through to the interior. The *Luftwaffe* (German air force) quickly established air mastery. The tanks swept on, surrounding towns in pincer movements, unrelentingly advancing on Paris.

French defences

The French army was as big as the Wehrmacht, and had even more tanks. The ten divisions of the British Expeditionary Force had crossed the English Channel to help out, just as in 1914. Above them flew such modern Hawker Hurricane fighter aircraft as Britain's Royal Air Force (RAF) could spare, as well as obsolete Fairey Battle bombers; these were easy targets for the Luftwaffe.

Dunkirk

All through May, Allied forces were beaten back. British commanders, believing that the French could not support them any more, withdrew their troops to Dunkirk, a port on the French coast. Hitler now had the British at his mercy. But then, amazingly, he ordered a halt. This decision, unwillingly obeyed, enabled a huge rescue operation to take place which, to the British people at least, has always possessed the qualities of heroic mythology.

An emergency appeal went out to owners of small boats along England's south coast. From 26 May nearly a thousand fishing craft, motor launches and pleasure steamers crossed the Channel: by 3 June they had rescued 338,000 Allied troops.

But the French were angry. They had held the German advance up at Lille and they wanted to fight on. Instead they had to watch British soldiers being rescued while they were left behind. Finally, 50,000 French troops were taken off, but only after British forces had been evacuated. To the French, Dunkirk was a betrayal.

Elite German SS troops strike a casual pose for a photograph during the invasion of France.

On 14 June the German army entered Paris and marched down the Champs Elysées. On 22 June France surrendered. An armistice was signed in the very railway carriage in which Germany's surrender of 1918 took place. Hitler's revenge was complete.

Aftermath

Marshal Pétain, hero of Verdun, was persuaded to be the new French president. A government of Nazi sympathisers – the Vichy regime – was set up.

But underground resistance movements sprang up as well, notably the *Maquis*. General de Gaulle escaped to England and set up the Free French army. Already, the seeds of eventual German defeat were being sown.

The remnants of the British army were home. Britain had a breathing space.

● German Messerschmitt Me109 fighter, deadly and effective in the Battle of Britain.

Germany prepared an invasion force – Operation Sealion – along the French coast. Hermann Goering, chief of the Luftwaffe, promised to destroy the RAF. The Battle of Britain was about to begin.

RAF's Fighter Command had 900 fighters, mainly new Spitfires and Hurricanes, but the pilots were raw and inexperienced in combat. The Luftwaffe had many more fighters, mostly deadly Messerschmitt Me109s, and over a thousand bombers.

Direction finding

By 1939 Germany had better radar than Britain, yet German commanders never worked out why the RAF was always ready and waiting for them. A chain of Radio Direction Finding (RDF) stations on the English coast gave early warning of the Luftwaffe's approach, allowing the RAF's fighters to take off at once.

War in the skies

In June 1940 the Luftwaffe started attacking Channel shipping to clear the sea for the invasion of Britain, but by July Operation Sealion was in difficulties. In August German attacks concentrated on airfields, but they met stiff resistance and lost more planes than the RAF. Even so, several airfields, such as Biggin Hill, in Kent, were devastated.

Hitler became impatient. In September, Goering ordered raids on London and other cities. Now the RAF used the "Big Wing", hundreds of fighters ready in the air to meet the Luftwaffe. The last big raid was on 15 September, "Battle of Britain Day". So many German planes were lost that Hitler decided to postpone Operation Sealion in order to attack Russia.

The Blitz

Winston Churchill coined the phrase "Battle of Britain": a titanic campaign waged by a few brave men that saved the nation. But to Germany it was merely a withdrawal because the RAF had not been destroyed. Now Hitler tried to defeat Britain with mass aerial bombing raids on factories, transport and cities, known as the "Blitz", the German word for lightning.

Defences

At first, British cities were poorly protected from aerial attack, with insufficient anti-aircraft guns and ineffective searchlights. The RAF had few night-fighters. However, this situation gradually began to improve.

The Air Raid Warden shouting, "Put that light out!" had become almost a joke. But it was no joke when the Blitz started. They, volunteer fire watchers and the fire and ambulance services did wonderful work dealing with the carnage left by every raid.

The air raids

Night raids on London lasted from September to November 1940. Every night hundreds of enemy bombers dropped high-explosive bombs and incendiaries, which spread fire. People took cover in air-raid shelters, but were safer when they could sleep in Underground stations. Morale was not broken, even in the biggest raid of all on 15 October.

In mid-November, other British cities were hit, including the mass raid on Coventry, which destroyed the centre of the city and its historic cathedral.

In 1941 ports were targeted, but British defences were now more advanced: the RAF had radar-equipped aircraft, better searchlights and accurate anti-aircraft guns.

Eventually, Hitler began to look eastwards. He planned to invade Russia before winter set in, and the first Blitz on Britain ended.

Across the Atlantic, the American people watched and wondered if they could do more than supply weapons.

"Never in the field of human conflict was so much owed by so many to so few."

Winston Churchill on the RAF, 1940

Vapour trails from aerial battles criss-cross the sky above St. Paul's Cathedral, London, during

Now came Hitler's greatest gamble and the most vicious, titanic campaign of the Second World War.

Even though he and Joseph Stalin had signed a non-aggression pact in 1939, Hitler always intended to invade the Soviet Union. To the east there was living space for the Aryan people, the Ukrainian wheatlands and the oil of the Caucasus region. Above all there was communism, which Hitler detested and wished to destroy.

Surprise attack

Hitler wanted a quick campaign. Soviet troops were not ready, the Wehrmacht was far better equipped and Stalin suspected nothing. Four million soldiers, including allies such as Italians and Romanians, were ready. War was to be waged ruthlessly, as that against Poland had been. Slavs were *Untermenschen*: "ruthless Germanisation" and genocide were in Hitler's mind.

The onslaught, named Operation Barbarossa, started on 22 June 1941. By 11 July Hitler's troops were at the River Dnieper. In the north, Panzer groups threatened Smolensk, close to Moscow: to the south tanks in the Ukraine were poised to take Kiev. As they advanced they left behind complete destruction, killing Slavs and Jews as they went. It all seemed so easy. Hitler forecast victory in Moscow by the end of August.

The German advance through Russia was brutal, as this rare colour photograph shows.

Fightback

But Russia was about to rally. On 3 July 1941 Stalin announced "The Great Patriotic War". Though Smolensk and Kiev were encircled, the Soviet Red Army fought to the death. Resistance groups sprang up. Suddenly the Germans were far from home with an angry people around them and long supply lines to protect. Heavy rains came in August and September and bogged them down. Soon the Russian winter would freeze them in.

The gates of Moscow

The Germans now crawled forward slowly. Stalin declared Moscow a fortress, pulled all his forces back and ordered in reinforcements from Siberia. German generals in the field insisted their soldiers could not go on. Hitler ordered "a final effort of willpower." But cold, exhausted troops, taking huge losses, could not manage it.

By the New Year, Moscow was saved. Hitler, furious, dismissed Field Marshal von Brauchitscht and took command himself, though he didn't go and join his army at the gates of Moscow.

However, Barbarossa had been stopped. Moscow had beaten Hitler, just as it had beaten Napoleon 130 years before.

German troops advance behind their tanks in extreme Russian winter weather.

A German SS gun crew takes a break during the Russian campaign.

Japan was the most advanced country in the Pacific. From 1937 it had fought a weary, inconclusive war with China: by 1941 it looked south and west for expansion.

Britain, France and the Netherlands all had rich colonies in the Pacific region. To the east lay the mighty United States. But Japan believed that its people should control the Pacific area. Japanese-dominated "co-prosperity" was the aim.

Pearl Harbor

Pearl Harbor, in Hawaii, was the biggest US naval base in the Pacific. General Tojo, Japan's prime minister, believed that a lightning strike could destroy the entire US fleet. One raid could give Japan mastery of the Pacific.

On 22 November 1941 a strike force of aircraft carriers secretly set sail under cover of bad weather to a point less than 480 kilometres (300 miles) from Pearl Harbor. On 7 December the planes took off. The Americans were completely taken by surprise as wave after wave attacked. Battleships and destroyers at anchor were sunk. But, fearing counterattack, the Japanese did not touch dockyards and fuel tanks. The fleet was destroyed, but not the harbour.

USS *West Virginia*, ablaze and sinking during

The results

Japan had miscalculated. US aircraft carriers, the key to war in the Pacific, were safe at sea. Besides, Pearl Harbor brought the USA into the war in both the Pacific and in Europe. It was the ally Churchill had wished for since 1940.

War on two fronts

Now the Japanese waged war on two fronts. First, they planned a lightning conquest of British possessions in Asia. This included Burma, the gateway to India, Malaya, with its reserves of tin and rubber, and Singapore, the great trading port. Secondly, they aimed to destroy American bases on islands all over the Pacific.

War in the Pacific

On 8 December 1941 Japan invaded Malaya. On 14 December they entered Burma, starting a long battle to open the way to India. On 15 February 1942 Singapore fell. It was Britain's worst setback in the war.

Japan now started a furious assault on the American bases on the Philippines. General MacArthur's troops withdrew to Bataan, north of Manila. But US President Franklin D Roosevelt ordered MacArthur home. As MacArthur left, he vowed, "I shall return." Meanwhile his troops

British General Percival surrenders Singapore to General Yamashito of Japan in February 1942.

regrouped on the island of Corregidor and defended it desperately until it was taken.

Staring at the abyss

All over the Pacific, Japan was victorious. The Allies – Britain, the USA, Australia and New Zealand, with Indian, Burmese and Malayan troops – seemed powerless. General Tojo and his emperor seemed as unstoppable in the Pacific as Hitler was in Europe.

"December 7, 1941 – a date which will live in infamy."

US President FD Roosevelt, 8 December 1941

THE BATTLE OF THE ATLANTIC

1939-1943

If the Allies had lost the Battle of the Atlantic they would have lost the war. This gargantuan struggle by sea and air over the grey, stormy expanse of the Atlantic Ocean lasted throughout the war, though by 1943 it had effectively been won.

Cargo of death: a U-boat crew loads a torpedo.

U-boats and convoys

Just as in the First World War, Germany sought to starve Britain out by strangling its sea routes. After France fell Germany had access to ports ideal for U-boats (submarines): Brest and St Nazaire. The British had learnt the lessons of 1914-18: from the start, merchant ships sailed in convoys protected by the Navy.

From 1940 onwards came a long war of cat and mouse, with new threats gradually mastered, then succeeded by worse. By 1941, after Britain's Royal Navy sank the *Bismarck*, Germany's finest battleship, Germany almost ceased using surface ships: U-boats hunting in "wolf packs" became the scourge of the Allies.

At first they seemed to strike at will. Hundreds of merchant ships carrying precious cargoes of food and war materials went to the bottom of the sea – often with their entire crews – sunk by U-boat torpedoes. By 1941 the battle seemed lost. U-boat crews called this "the happy time".

The air gap

Gradually Allied navies found answers to the wolf packs. New bases were set up in Iceland. US and Canadian destroyers escorted convoys halfway across the Atlantic and the Royal Navy then took over. Air cover was given from the US and Britain. Where aircraft equipped with depth charges flew overhead the wolf packs were in danger. But aircraft had short ranges: in the middle of the ocean was the "air gap", where the convoys were sitting ducks for the U-boats.

The tide turns

As 1942 shaded into 1943, three vital elements hastened the defeat of the U-boats. The first was "Huff-duff" (high frequency direction finding), which could at last pinpoint U-boat positions. The second was the thin-winged Lockheed Liberator bomber, with a range long enough to plug the air gap. The third was when British code-breakers cracked secret German naval codes.

By May 1943 the Battle of the Atlantic was won. But it had been a hard, vicious, lonely time, and thousands of seamen had died terrible deaths, choking on oil and drowning in the cruel, cold Atlantic.

Another U-boat victim goes down. Often the entire ship's crew perished in the icy water.

For the Allies, control of the Mediterranean meant protection of the Suez Canal and the western entry to the Middle East and India. For Mussolini's fascist Italy it meant influence and expansion through capture of British possessions. For Germany it meant all these, plus protection of what Churchill called "the soft underbelly of Europe".

Oran and Taranto

Britain dared not allow French warships to fight as enemies. After Italy joined Germany in June 1940, Churchill ordered that French ships in Oran, a port in north-west Algeria – a French possession – should be destroyed. The Royal Navy obeyed the order with heavy heart. Then Britain mounted a daring attack on the Italian Navy at Taranto: ancient Fleet Air Arm Swordfish biplanes attacked in waves, sinking Italian warships at anchor. Japan learnt well from this for their attack on Pearl Harbor.

Greece, Tobruk and Crete

Mussolini's troops invaded Greece in October but the Greek army repelled them. However, their victory only meant that Germany would arrive sooner or later. Italy also invaded Egypt. With his small British force General Wavell attacked Mussolini's much bigger army at Sidi Barani. Completely victorious, he swept on to capture Tobruk. The British aimed to secure the whole of North Africa – until the Germans came.

On 6 April Germany invaded Greece and Yugoslavia. British troops rushed to their aid but could not stop the Germans and withdrew to Crete. In the first-ever airborne invasion, German paratroopers swarmed all over Crete while the Luftwaffe pounded it. Soon the British were defeated. Even so, Germany lost more troops than Britain: never again did they invade with paratroops alone.

Malta G.C.

This tiny island, Britain's only port between Egypt and Gibraltar, had just three old RAF Gladiator biplanes, "Faith", "Hope" and "Charity", to defend it. In June 1940 they somehow repelled the first air attacks by the Italian Air Force, but in 1941 raids by the Luftwaffe started. Though Malta's defences improved, the Luftwaffe dropped twice as many bombs as fell on London. The Maltese people suffered dreadfully. Aerial defences were strengthened but, though Royal Navy ships kept the island supplied, the population were nearly starved by

August 1941. Then Luftwaffe attacks, for a while, ceased. The Maltese people were collectively awarded Britain's George Cross medal for their fortitude. Meanwhile, German planes sank HMS *Ark Royal*, Britain's largest aircraft carrier. It was a grievous blow.

Rommel

In the spring of 1941 the German *Afrika Korps* (Africa Corps) landed in Libya. It was commanded by one of the most remarkable figures of the war – Field Marshal Erwin Rommel, also known as the "Desert Fox". His orders were to stiffen Italian defences but instead he attacked at once. The Afrika Korps swept east from Tripoli, recaptured Tobruk in June 1942 and started to drive the British back into Egypt. Cairo and Alexandria seemed at his mercy. Rommel was soon on the point of winning all of North Africa.

Field Marshal Erwin Rommel, the "Desert Fox", on the road to Cairo in 1942.

THE HOME FRONTS

The experience of war for people at home was different in each of the fighting countries. In some cases ordinary people were in as much danger as troops at the front line.

The Allies: Britain

Britain faced a time of bombing and blackouts, food, clothes and fuel rationing. Women joined the Army Territorial Service (ATS), the Women's Auxiliary Air Force (WAAF) and the Women's Royal Naval Service (WRNS, the "Wrens"). Thousands worked in factories building aeroplanes and making shells, or joined the Women's Land Army to help with farming. Men were exempt from military service if the work they did was vital to the war effort.

The Americans came in 1942: some women married "Yanks" and went to the USA as "G.I. Brides". Everyone relied on the "wireless" (radio) for news of the war and for entertainment. To many afterwards it seemed a happy, united time.

North America

In the United States and Canada the war was a time characterised by an extraordinary industrial effort: 300,000 planes, over fifty million tonnes of ships and innumerable tanks, guns and aircraft were built for the Allies. North Americans at home never faced a Blitz, though they always feared sabotage. Throughout North America there was a strong determination to pull together and see things through.

Occupied Europe

Citizens of these countries faced a great dilemma. Should they accept defeat and collaborate with the Germans, or keep up secret, dangerous resistance? It depended on who won the war as to who would be considered the traitors at the end.

In France the Maquis blew up bridges and railways and assassinated German soldiers, but often brought revenge on whole towns and villages. It was the same in Holland, Belgium,

A US dive-bomber aircraft assembly line.

Denmark, Norway, Eastern Europe and Russia.

Australia and New Zealand

Known then as Dominions, self-governing countries within the British Empire, they contributed hugely to the Allied war effort (the number of New Zealanders killed in relation to the population was proportionately the highest in the British Empire). However, home life was mostly unaffected, although Australia suffered Japanese air raids and invasion scares.

The Axis powers: Germany

When war came, most Germans, believing Nazi propaganda, were certain of victory. A united, disciplined society plunged into wholehearted service of the Third Reich. Young people joined the Hitler Youth. Later they flocked into the services. Until 1942 morale remained sky-high. But as the war turned, Germans endured huge suffering. Allied bomber aircraft rained havoc, far greater than Germany had wrought on Britain.

Many lost faith in Hitler. Resistance grew: in 1944 a failed assassination plot saw many executions. But many Germans remained stubbornly resolute, even when their country was overrun by the Allies.

Italy

As a fascist dictator who said he would "make the trains run on time", Mussolini led a country which never really took to war. Many Italians saw through Mussolini - the "sawdust Caesar". Despite rationing most people thrived on the black market and tried to lead carefree lives. But after Mussolini surrendered in 1943, Italian resistance to Germany was just as brave – and as savagely punished – as any in the rest of Europe.

Japan

The strength and determination of the Japanese people came from loyalty to traditional values – service and love of the emperor. Japanese people stoically put up with misery and near-starvation with intense, sometimes fanatic, patriotism and love of country, until they suffered the single most defining act of the twentieth century – the first atomic bomb.

"Just as we struggle, so you must work for victory!" says the heroic soldier on a German propaganda poster.

CAPTURE AND ESCAPE

It was the POW's duty to escape if he could: some break-outs were famously successful.

Prisoners of war – Europe

Many servicemen on both sides were taken prisoner. The experiences of prisoners of war (POWs) in Europe were different from those in the Pacific. Enemy prisoners in Britain were on an island from which

> **"It is the duty of all captured officers to try and escape."**
>
> British forces official regulation

escape was hard. Many were allowed out of their camps to work on farms. Some even stayed after the war and married British women.

Prisoners of war – the Far East

European countries believed that a soldier taken prisoner was out of the war and merited humane treatment. The Japanese view of POWs was different. Soldiers should die rather than be captured – there were few Japanese POWs. The Japanese despised Allied prisoners, providing them with minimal food and shelter, summary executions and hard work, most infamously on the Burma Railway: the "railway of death" in the film *Bridge on the River Kwai*.

The camps

For able-bodied Jews and *Untermenschen* in occupied countries, the prospect was the forced labour camp where prisoners were worked till they dropped. For women and children, the aged and infirm it was the concentration camp or the Death Camps. These gave up their terrible secrets of genocide and the true nature of Hitler's "Final Solution" at the war's end (see pages 34-35).

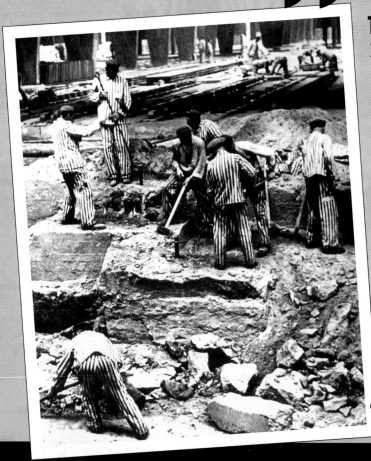

Wearing the striped uniform of the concentration camp, political prisoners toil to construct a Berlin war factory.

War is not just a matter of armies, navies and air forces. There is another level: spies, code-breaking and underground resistance. In the Second World War it was to prove decisive.

The German Enigma code machine

SOE (Special Operations Executive)

All countries had their Secret Services: SOE was the name of the British version. It trained secret agents who were later parachuted into occupied countries to work with resistance groups. Agents were equipped with forged papers and knowledge of sabotage. Their work was dangerous, often leading to capture and execution, but what they did in encouraging and motivating Resistance groups was vital.

ENIGMA

ENIGMA was the German cipher machine. It generated infinite numbers of codes and the Germans thought it was unbreakable. But it was not. It was read by Polish code-breakers as early as 1932, by the French in 1938 and the British in 1940.

In 1941, a British naval officer and a sailor later found to be too young to serve retrieved an Enigma machine from a sinking U-boat: from then on the Allies had a huge advantage. Messages deciphered at Bletchley Park in Buckinghamshire gave advance warning of U-boat positions, army movements and air force strengths. Without this information the Allies might well have been defeated.

MAGIC was the US codeword for deciphering Japanese coded messages after they broke into a Japanese machine similar to Enigma, codenamed PURPLE.

Deception

Both sides employed deception and tried to detect the others doing it. There is a story, possibly untrue, that the Germans built dummy U-boat pens out of wood to deceive the RAF, who found out and raided them with wooden bombs. More importantly, Germany thought that the D-Day landings would be near Calais because photographs showed a huge build-up of forces in eastern England. These, however, were dummies.

In 1942, with Britain seemingly defeated in south-east Asia, the USA led Allied efforts in the Pacific. General Douglas MacArthur commanded land forces; Admiral Chester Nimitz led the US Navy.

The carrier USS *Yorktown* sinks after the Battle of Midway in 1942.

The Doolittle Raid

Shocked by Pearl Harbor, President Roosevelt asked for a revenge air raid on Japan. Under Colonel Doolittle, volunteer bomber crews were to make a night raid. But the US fleet was discovered. The bombers had to take off from aircraft carriers by day, on 18 April. Some of the raid's effect was thus lost, as were most of the bombers, though many crews baled out over China or Russia. However, a few were captured by the Japanese and executed. Even so, the Doolittle Raid improved US morale.

Midway

The next Japanese objective to break US power was to attack the naval base on the island of Midway, 965 kilometres (600 miles) west of Hawaii. On 4 June 1942, waves of Japanese bombers struck. Once again, US aircraft carriers were targeted. But the Americans had had warning: the carriers were waiting in ambush. US planes destroyed four Japanese aircraft carriers. Only one US carrier, the USS *Yorktown*, was sunk. At last, the USA had defeated Japan in battle.

Guadalcanal

Guadalcanal is a hot, steamy island in the Solomon Islands, about 965 kilometres (600 miles) east of New Guinea. For six months beginning in August 1942 it was the scene of one of the bitterest battles in the Pacific War. There was already a Japanese base there with an unfinished airfield. The first US landing was small; it met little opposition until the Japanese sent in a much superior force. In danger of losing aircraft carriers, the US withdrew. The Marines had to repel the Japanese as best they could.

Fight for Henderson Field

Possession of Henderson Field, the airstrip on Guadalcanal, was vital. The US Marines faced many desperate enemy attacks, but gradually they managed to break out. Meanwhile, at sea, vast battles were fought. Several US carriers were sunk; Japan seemed to be winning. But in October the US fleet went on the offensive and slowly regained the advantage.

On land, the Japanese poured troops in to dislodge the Marines. They pounded Henderson Field with big naval guns from out at sea. But the Americans held on. On 12 November the Japanese attempted to land their best troops, the 38th Division, to strike a decisive blow. But now a three-day naval battle started.

Ships were sunk on both sides but the Japanese landing was stopped and the landing craft destroyed. Finally the Americans were winning.

By now, the reinforced US troops far outnumbered the Japanese. Still the Japanese troops fought with fanatical bravery. They refused to surrender but died where they stood, taking their opponents with them. Fighting continued, on land and sea and in the air, until the end of January 1943 when the remaining Japanese soldiers were taken off the island in a daring night operation the Americans knew nothing about until it was over.

Guadalcanal was the real turning point in the Pacific. From now on, the Allies were on the attack.

US Marines storm ashore at Guadalcanal.

THE TIDE TURNS IN NORTH AFRICA

When Rommel recaptured Tobruk it seemed nothing could stop him forcing the British out of Egypt.

But in July 1942 General Auchinleck's 8th Army, the "Desert Rats", faced the Afrika Korps at the first battle of El Alamein and held them up. Even so, Churchill was not pleased with how things were going in North Africa. He replaced Auchinleck as Commander-in-Chief and put General Bernard Montgomery at the head of the 8th Army.

The second battle of El Alamein

Rommel suspected that an attack was coming. The Afrika Korps was short of petrol and he knew he could not fight the war of movement he preferred so he ordered unbreachable defences to be built. Thousands of anti-tank mines were laid, called "the devil's gardens", to slow the British advance. He stationed his big guns and had his infantry ready to break out.

Montgomery would never attack without having superior forces. For the first time in North Africa, the British were stronger. Montgomery's main thrust was where the Afrika Korps was strongest, and Rommel was taken by surprise. On 23 October British artillery opened up in a

British infantry charge an enemy position at El Alamein during October 1942.

ferocious bombardment. The British advance was slow but Rommel's counter-attacks failed. Australian and New Zealand infantry advanced, paving the way for Allied tanks. By 4 November Rommel was beaten, and his troops withdrew. War in North Africa – and indeed war in the west – had reached its turning point.

Operation Torch

The 8th Army now began to push Rommel westwards. On 8 November American and British troops led by

US General Dwight D Eisenhower landed in Algeria – a French colony governed by the Vichy regime – in what was known as Operation Torch.

The Allies hoped that French troops would fight on their side. But the Vichyites refused and the French fought against the Allies. Admiral Darlan, the Vichy commander, only gave in when things were hopeless.

Tunisia

The Allies pushed on, against newly reinforced German and Italian troops under General Arnim. He and Rommel disliked each other and ruined Axis resistance with their disagreements. In March 1943, Rommel – who was ill – was recalled to Germany. Allied troops withstood several ineffective attacks, but Montgomery's 8th Army was coming westwards fast. The final battle took place at Tunis. On 13 May Axis resistance crumbled. North Africa was safe and the Allies looked out towards Sicily and then Italy.

Sicily and Italy

The landings in Sicily took place on 10 July 1943. The island was captured by 12 August, but not before 100,000 Axis troops with their equipment had been evacuated to the mainland. However, by this time Italy was out of the war. On 25 July 1943 Mussolini had been thrown out of office, so an invasion of Italy seemed the next step. But it was a bitter struggle for the Allies. The battle for Monte Cassino resembled the fighting in the trenches of the First World War. German General Kesselring's troops fought a stubborn defensive campaign. No Allied objectives – to reach Austria and the south of France or to help Russia – were achieved.

After the D-Day landings in Normandy in 1944, the Italian campaign dragged on while more important events happened elsewhere.

The front cover of YANK, the wartime magazine for US troops, shows the ruins of Monte Cassino's historic medieval monastery.

Soviet troops engaged in bitter fighting at Stalingrad.

Stalingrad – attack

The city stood on the River Volga. Beyond it, Asia beckoned. On 12 September 1942, the first German troops entered Stalingrad. Stalin put Marshal Timoshenko in charge of Russian troops and poured reinforcements in. On 25 September the communist party headquarters fell. Surely, people thought, Stalingrad must fall with it.

But now the real Soviet resistance was starting. Soldiers and civilians were holed up in houses, shops and cellars. Every rooftop had snipers. As the Wehrmacht led by General von Paulus advanced deeper into the city there were desperate hand-to-hand battles.

After a month, the Germans had virtually nothing to show for their fighting. The second hard Russian winter of their campaign was setting in. The River Volga began to freeze. Had the Germans gone too far?

All through 1941 and 1942, German troops swept through the Ukraine, leaving terror and destruction behind them. They aimed for the oilfields of the Caucasus region only to find that the Russians had destroyed them. But the city of Stalingrad (now Volgograd) faced them. For Joseph Stalin to lose the city bearing his name was something he would not tolerate.

"Za Stalina! Za Rodinu!"
("For Stalin! For the Motherland!")

Soviet battle slogan at Stalingrad

Counter-attack

Hitler was already wondering whether he had bitten off more than he could chew. The North African situation was serious. He ordered his transport planes to Tunis. In Russia, von Paulus's troops were short of ammunition and food. In November the Red Army to the north attacked after a massive artillery bombardment. The following day, more Russians attacked from the south: the Germans were trapped.

Von Paulus urged Hitler to let him retreat, but Hitler ordered them to fight to the last man. Von Paulus's position was hopeless. His men were suffering greatly: he was not able, as a good general should, to help them.

On 31 January 1943, a propaganda broadcast to the German people declared Stalingrad a great victory for the Third Reich. On the same day, von Paulus surrendered. Hitler's Soviet campaign was foundering.

Kursk

Kursk, 800 kilometres (500 miles) south of Moscow, was an important transport junction. The Red Army still held it, though there were Germans to the north and south. In July 1943, Hitler ordered Operation Citadel, to capture Kursk, surround the Russians and finish them off. A huge tank force was assembled. But Stalin and his army chiefs saw the danger. Huge masses of tanks faced each other – 2,500 German, 3,400 Russian.

On 12 July the 2nd SS Panzer Corps met the Soviet 5th Guards Tank Army. This was the largest tank battle of the war, and probably ever. The 2nd Panzer Corps was Germany's best. But Hitler ordered them to withdraw from Kursk so he could repel British and American forces landing in Sicily and Italy. The battle for Kursk raged on, but now the USSR had gained the upper hand.

A German soldier lies dead beside a burning tank at Kursk, 1943.

Since Barbarossa began in 1941, the Allies had wondered how to help the Soviets when they were not able to open a second front in the west themselves. The answer seemed clear: aerial bombing.

The beginnings

The Blitz had taught the Allies a lot. Mass bombing could work, though at a cost. Britain might have crumbled if Hitler had kept it up. It hadn't broken the people's spirit, but perhaps it might if more bombs had been dropped for a longer period from bigger, heavier bomber aircraft.

Bomber Command

First, there must be better bombers. Four-engined aeroplanes were introduced: the Stirling, Halifax and, most effective, the Lancaster. These had longer ranges and carried heavier bomb loads. But no fighter aircraft had sufficient range to escort and defend them over Germany. There was only one answer to this: night raids, even though aircrews wouldn't be able to see the targets.

The USAAF

When the United States Army Air Force arrived in Britain they had a different answer – the Boeing B-17 "Flying Fortress" bomber. These were designed to carry out daylight raids,

An aerial view of an RAF Lancaster dropping its bombs over the target.

People in Dresden flee from the firestorm during Allied night bombing in 1945.

RAF de Havilland Mosquito fighter-bomber aircraft in formation. The "Mozzie's" airframe was made of wood.

so they could attack single targets more precisely. However, because daylight raids meant that they could easily be attacked by enemy fighters, B-17s were more heavily armed than RAF bombers.

Area bombing

To the British, mass bombing of city centres by night seemed the best policy. When Air Vice-Marshall Arthur "Bomber" Harris was put in charge of Bomber Command he mounted the first "thousand bomber raid" on Cologne. It seemed a huge success and from now on, this was the RAF's main weapon. But German air defences were strong. Many RAF planes were lost; 50,000 airmen died. Often the raids were inaccurate: it took the "Pathfinder" squadrons and the de Havilland Mosquito fighter-bomber equipped with "Oboe", the first radar-guided precision bombing system, to make them effective.

There were morale-boosting triumphs such as the 1943 Dambusters raid on the Mohne, Eder and Sorpe dams. But some events cast a cloud over Bomber Harris's reputation, such as the 1945 firebombing of Dresden, when the city was destroyed by a huge firestorm.

The Mustang

In 1944 the first long-range fighter, the Mustang, was introduced. It was a US design but had a powerful British Rolls-Royce Merlin engine. At last bombers could penetrate deep into German territory with adequate fighter cover to protect them. German resistance became weaker, and after D-Day in 1944 Bomber Command and the USAAF concentrated on helping the invasion of Europe.

The results

The Allies' bombing offensive had severely damaged Germany, though at immense cost to the Allied forces. The old doctrine that "the bomber will always get through" was not necessarily true. But the lessons of strategic bombing have dominated most wars fought ever since.

All dictators look to scapegoats for their country's ills. When he came to power, Hitler settled on the Jewish people. He was determined to eliminate Jews and all other so-called *Untermenschen* from Germany and eventually from all German possessions.

He called the Jews degenerates, not true Germans, parasites holding the country to ransom. He inflamed the German people against them. He took away the civil rights of the Jewish population and incited mobs to destroy their property.

One night in November 1938 Jewish shops were ransacked and looted. Because of the sound of breaking windows all over Germany, the night came to be known as *Kristallnacht* (night of the broken glass). Many Jews fled the country. Special trains of the *Kindertransport* (children's transport) took thousands of Jewish children to safety in Britain. Other Jews were sent to concentration camps.

Massacres

Starting with Poland in 1939, Jews were murdered in every country Hitler entered. First came mass killings: hundreds shot at a time or herded into synagogues, locked in and burnt alive.

But such massacres took time. Hitler ordered ghettos to be set up. These were closed-off areas where Jews had to live in appalling conditions and work until they dropped. In this way, cities could be declared *Judenfrei* (Jew-free). The more countries Germany invaded, the more Jews there were to get rid of. The *Einsatzgruppen* were set up. These were murder squads charged solely with killing Jews. At Babi Yar, near Kiev, over thirty thousand Jews were killed in three days.

Many Germans were deeply troubled by such brutality. So Hitler began to think of another way to wipe out the Jews, one that people would not find out about.

The "Final Solution"

Adolf Eichmann was charged by Hitler with planning a terrible "Final Solution" to the "Jewish question". By 1942 he had worked it out. Jews were to be "resettled", taken first to holding camps, then by train to special camps far away in Eastern Europe. Even the train crews had no idea what they were taking their passengers to.

There were several such camps; one of most notorious was Treblinka in Poland. Here, mass murder was carried out with inhuman efficiency.

Hundreds of victims at a time were herded naked into rooms marked "Showers". But these rooms were not for washing. They were locked in and poison gas poured through the ceilings. When everyone was dead their bodies were loaded into incinerators – after their gold teeth had been removed. Nearly one million Jews were murdered in this way at Treblinka.

At another camp, Auschwitz, millions went to the gas chambers but thousands more also died working in coal mines and factories. Still others were murdered by the camp guards or killed in brutal "medical experiments". Some were sent back to Germany, to camps such as Belsen and Dachau, where they were used as slave labour. Here, in 1945, the Allies discovered them. And at last the world found

Survivors of Auschwitz stare blankly from behind the barbed wire.

out about the Holocaust, the Nazi Party's greatest crime and the worst genocide of all time.

In 1943, Winston Churchill and Franklin D Roosevelt met in Casablanca, North Africa to begin planning the invasion of Europe and its liberation from Nazi occupation.

On 19 August 1942, a raid on the French port of Dieppe by a force comprised of mainly Canadian soldiers tested out German defences. It was a disaster, with heavy casualties, but it showed how difficult a seaborne invasion of occupied Europe would be.

Planning

Operation Overlord, or D-Day, as it became known, was set up under General Eisenhower. The port of Cherbourg, in Normandy, was to be captured. Amphibious landings were planned on the beaches between Cherbourg and Le Havre. Once landed, troops would be supplied from huge artificial harbours constructed off the French coast and fuel oil pumped ashore through undersea pipelines.

Huge concentrations of Allied troops and weapons began to arrive in southern England. Landing craft and troop-carrying gliders were assembled. The invasion force was going to be the biggest the world had ever seen.

German defences

Hitler knew an invasion would come, but had no idea where, though he assumed it would take the shortest route across the Channel, to Calais. Rommel, now in charge of the army in the west, disagreed. The whole Channel coast was strengthened, in spite of heavy Allied air raids.

Operation Fortitude

What the Germans didn't realise was that they were being fooled, and that a huge campaign of deception – Operation Fortitude – was being staged by the Allies. Massive army installations were put in place in Kent. But the tanks that were visible to German reconnaissance aircraft were inflatable, and buildings were constructed from wood and canvas. Fake coded messages were sent out to deliberately filter misinformation through to the enemy. As a result, the Germans believed the invasion, when it came, would be near Calais.

The Normandy landings

D-Day was set for 5 June 1944 but a storm blew up. The next day the weather was no better. However, Eisenhower ordered the invasion force to set sail. A huge force of landing craft packed with British, Canadian and US soldiers set sail for Normandy, protected by naval and air cover. Earlier that morning, paratroops had landed and were busy destroying bridges and cutting railways and roads, continuing the work of the French Resistance, which had been busy for months.

By 6.30 am American troops were landing on beaches code-named "Utah" and "Omaha". British and Canadians landed on "Gold", "Juno" and "Sword". Resistance was fierce, but by evening the Allies were ashore and had established beachheads. Fewer than five thousand men were killed – a lower number than had been feared. But a hard, vicious battle was about to start.

V-weapons

Wernher von Braun, a German scientist, perfected the V- (for Vengeance) weapons, pilotless flying bombs, to Blitz Britain a second time. The campaign was delayed by D-Day.

The missiles caused panic in London, but gradually the RAF got the better of them. In September 1944 fearsome supersonic V-2 rockets began to come over, suddenly and without warning. There was no defence against them – only concentrated air raids on their launching site could stop them, until Allied troops eventually captured it.

D-Day 6 June 1944: US troops in their landing craft head for Omaha Beach.

Breaking out of Normandy was difficult. By 27 June US troops had captured Cherbourg, but a storm held up supplies for several days.

A battle for the city of Caen lasted until well into July 1944: when Allied armies tried to break out of Normandy they were trapped at Falaise by advancing German forces driving a wedge between them. Now the bitterest fighting took place. Over a hundred British tanks were lost – one-third of their force in France – and four thousand men were killed.

Gradually, however, the Allies closed the "Falaise Gap", as Americans from the south and Canadians from the north cut off the German forces that had advanced westwards. By 20 August the Gap was closed and the Germans utterly defeated.

Liberation of Paris

Now the Allies could move eastwards, and all Paris knew they were coming. Resistance leaders ordered an uprising and barricades went up all over the city. The Germans hesitated to crush the uprising, not wanting to repeat the carnage in Warsaw when the Poles rose up against them, only to be let down by Soviet forces delaying their advance on the city. Nothing would now delay the Allies: Paris had to be saved.

On 25 August, General Leclerc's French troops entered the city and the occupiers surrendered. The road to Germany seemed open.

Arnhem

The Allies' next main objective was the Belgian port of Antwerp and control of the River Scheldt estuary. On 4 September General Montgomery's tanks reached Antwerp. But across the banks of the River Scheldt the Germans stood firm. Then Montgomery made his biggest mistake of the war.

Montgomery believed that if he could put troops on the other side of the River Rhine at Arnhem and cut the Germans off he could drive straight for the heart of Germany, so on 17 September Operation Market Garden started. Paratroops were to capture the Rhine bridges; then the infantry could cross the river and

A snowed-in US tank in the Battle of the Bulge.

secure the bridgehead. But unknown to the Allies, two Panzer divisions were nearby. American airborne troops landed safely, but British troops ended up too far away. The Germans were able to cut off the British forces, tie the Americans down and destroy the bridges over the Rhine. The attack was a brave failure. Many men were lost and the Allied advance was slowed.

Battle of the Bulge

In 1940, Hitler had invaded France through the thickly wooded Ardennes region, surprising the French. In December 1944 his last gamble was to take the Allies by surprise with a similar offensive.

Every available Panzer division was assembled; the Allies were deceived into thinking they were only there for defence. In October the

Americans had captured their first German city, Aachen, and pressed on, leaving the Ardennes lightly defended.

On 16 December, in fog and half-darkness, the Germans attacked and beat the Americans back. The situation was desperate until the weather cleared and Allied planes could take off again. However, by Christmas Eve German supply lines were shattered and German forces were isolated. Only heavy snow allowed survivors to make an escape.

By the New Year this "Battle of the Bulge" (the "bulge" was the pocket in the Allied front line caused by the German offensive) was over. The way into Germany really was clear.

"We can still lose this war."

US General Patton warns the Allies during the Battle of the Bulge

THE RACE TO BERLIN
1945

By January 1945 German troops were in full retreat on both eastern and western fronts.

The Allies crossed the Rhine and the Russians crossed the Oder, not 80 kilometres (50 miles) from Berlin. The Wehrmacht kept fighting desperately all the way, with even sixteen-year-old boys in the front line. But they could not check the race to conquer Hitler's capital city.

At the gates of Berlin

All through March and April, his senior commanders urged Hitler to surrender. He refused. On 1 April he took refuge in a bunker deep beneath his Chancellery in Berlin. His people had no fuel or ammunition left to fight a war, the Russians were at the gates of Berlin, the Allies had overrun the Ruhr region and nearly all German industry with it, but still Hitler would not give up.

When US President Roosevelt died suddenly on 15 April Hitler

The capture of Berlin: Soviet planes fly over the Reichstag (German parliament building) as tanks advance.

40

seemed to think the war would turn in his favour. On 20 April he celebrated his birthday. On 25 April American and Russian troops met at the River Elbe and their commanders shook hands.

On 28 April, Red Army troops were in Berlin while in Italy, partisans freed Mussolini from prison, shot him and hung his body upside down in a street in Milan.

The death of Hitler

Hitler's Third Reich, meant to last "a thousand years", was doomed after a mere twelve. On 30 April he sent his personal staff away and shot himself. His wife, Eva Braun, poisoned herself. When Red Army soldiers entered the bunker they found their petrol-soaked bodies still burning. On 2 May Berlin surrendered.

Final surrender

For some days, German troops fought on, though they knew their cause was hopeless. Then, on 3 May German forces in Holland, Belgium, Denmark and northern Germany surrendered to Montgomery on Luneberg Heath. On 5 May German troops in Norway surrendered. On 7 May General Jödl, Chief of the Operations Staff of the German High Command, signed the formal surrender of all German troops in Europe. The war in Europe was over after five long, weary years.

General Montgomery meets the German surrender party on Luneberg Heath on 3 May 1945.

VE Day

Victory in Europe Day in Britain and North America was declared on 8 May. Scenes of wild rejoicing broke out. In London, thousands crowded outside Buckingham Palace to see King George VI, Queen Elizabeth and Prime Minister Winston Churchill on the balcony of Buckingham Palace. But in Germany there was devastation and terrible fear for the future.

“
"East and West have met . . . the forces of liberation have joined hands."

Radio commentator, 25 April 1945

Throughout 1944 US forces took island after island, pushing the Japanese back. General MacArthur recaptured the Philippines, proclaiming, "I have returned." 1945 dawned. The final hours were close.

Iwo Jima

This island, 965 kilometres (600 miles) from Japan, was equipped with airstrips vital to Japan's defence. After three months of heavy bombing, US Marines landed on 9 February 1945. Another bitter battle ensued. For five weeks Japanese troops fought with fanatic bravery until their last stand in a rocky valley, known afterwards as "Bloody Gorge".

Okinawa

Another island, 560 kilometres (350 miles) south of Japan, Okinawa was also key to the defence of Japan. An invasion force nearly as large as that used for D-Day was needed to capture it. A huge army hid in caves and rocks: fearsome obstacles littered the beaches. US ships faced *Kamikaze* (suicide) attacks. Both sides lost thousands of men in the hard and bloody battle which lasted from 1 April to 22 June. On that day Usijima Mitsuru, the Japanese general, committed suicide. The Allies had crossed the last barrier to Japan.

The super-battleship USS *Missouri*, which was launched in January 1944, and which took part in the closing stages of the Pacific war.

The atomic bomb

Scientists had known for some years that splitting the atom could release vast energy, which could be used as a devastating weapon. Britain, the USA, Russia and Germany were racing to see who could develop it first. German efforts were well advanced. In 1941, British and American efforts were combined in the Manhattan Project at Los Alamos, New Mexico. By May 1945 Germany was defeated. In July 1945 an atomic bomb was successfully tested near Los Alamos.

The siege of Japan

On 9 March US aircraft started intensive bombing raids with incendiaries all over mainland Japan. City after city suffered grievous damage. Japanese people waited for the expected invasion but it never came.

Hiroshima and Nagasaki

American troops were poised to invade. On the mainland, the Soviet Red Army was ready to join them. But already the strains were showing: the Americans did not want Russian influence in Japan. A fateful decision was taken. On the morning of 6 August a single B-29 Superfortress aircraft, accompanied by weather planes, took off from the Pacific island of Tinian. When it was over the city of Hiroshima it dropped "Little Boy", the first atom bomb used in anger. Hiroshima was completely destroyed. For the first time, the world saw the dreaded mushroom cloud and learned what radiation was. On 9 August a second bomb was dropped on Nagasaki. On the same day, Russia declared war on Japan. On 14 August Japanese Emperor Hirohito surrendered. The Second World War was over.

Almost nothing remained of Hiroshima after the atomic bomb explosion of 6 August 1945.

The atomic bombing of Hiroshima changed the world. Nuclear power now determined the future. Virtually everything that has happened since depends in some way on the fear of its terrifying destructive power.

Potsdam

At Potsdam in July 1945, Attlee, Truman and Stalin decided on a way forward. Germany and Japan would be treated sympathetically. War criminals would meet justice but the countries themselves would be rebuilt. The errors of Versailles were not to be repeated. But how each victor interpreted this agreement determined the next fifty years.

The immediate aftermath

At a conference in February 1945 in the Russian town of Yalta, Churchill, Roosevelt and Stalin decided Germany's future – division into four zones of occupation, American, British, French and Russian. However, by the time Japan surrendered, there were changes in Britain and the US. Roosevelt was dead and President Harry S Truman had succeeded him. Churchill had been beaten in a general election: the new prime minister was a member of the Labour party named Clement Attlee. Of the Allied leaders only Joseph Stalin survived the war in charge.

The United Nations

As early as 1941 the Allies had drawn up the Atlantic Charter, forming the Grand Alliance against the Axis powers. In 1944 the Dumbarton Oaks conference in the USA set up a United Nations Organisation and the International Court of Justice. In April 1945, at the San Francisco conference, the United Nations started, with a permanent home at Lake Success, near New York. It was a League of Nations, but it had teeth.

The Nuremberg Trials

In October 1945, the captured Nazis met their fates under stringent cross-examination and judgement. Goering, von Ribbentrop, Keitel and several others were sentenced to death as war criminals. Hess was gaoled for life. Others received long sentences; three were acquitted.

"We have learned that we cannot live alone, at peace; that our own well-being is dependent on the well-being of other nations far away."

FD Roosevelt in his 1945 inaugural address

The Cold War begins

It was Churchill who first coined the phrase the "Iron Curtain" to describe the division of Europe into the free western nations and communist eastern nations. This set the boundaries of the Cold War: crucially, the boundary ran through Germany.

The USA and the USSR were now the world's superpowers and an arms race began. Each side strove for larger and more destructive nuclear capacities and justified this huge and dangerous expenditure on the need to deter the other. A Third World War, of unthinkable ferocity, seemed inevitable.

Germany and Japan, now democracies, were gradually incorporated as allies; the North Atlantic Treaty Organisation (NATO) was set up between North America and Europe.

The Berlin Airlift

In June 1948 it seemed as though World War Three was starting. The USSR, which controlled the part of Germany surrounding Berlin, cut all communications to the city. For a year the zones of Berlin controlled by the western Allies had to be supplied by air. In 1949, however, the USSR called off the blockade and the separate nations of East and West Germany evolved. This situation lasted until the reunification of Germany in 1990.

Israel and the Middle East

In 1917 Arthur Balfour, British Prime Minister, declared that there should be a Jewish homeland in Palestine. At the end of the Second World War, when the world learned of the Holocaust, this seemed pressing. In 1948 the state of Israel was founded: a direct result of the Second World War. Its effect on the present world situation has been profound.

The European Community

Another concept Winston Churchill expressed was a "United States of Europe" to prevent future European wars. That has remained the EU's basic purpose. The reconciliation of former enemies into a great mutual self-help organisation seems at last to have lifted the curse of the last millennium on Europe.

Nazi leaders Herman Goering (top left) and Rudolf Hess on trial for war crimes at Nuremberg, 1945-46.

GLOSSARY

Allies Britain and its Empire, the USA, USSR, France and China: the countries which fought against the Axis powers.

Aircraft carrier A fighting ship designed to act as a floating airbase.

Air raid An attack by bomber aircraft on targets, which might be military but might also be civilian, such as the German Blitz and the Allied bombing campaign.

Air-raid shelter A structure – either specially built or makeshift – to protect people during air raids.

Artillery The big guns used in warfare on land.

Axis powers The name for countries allied to Germany, so called after the treaty between Hitler and Mussolini in 1936 which set up the "Rome-Berlin Axis".

Blitzkrieg "Lightning War" – an attack with speed, surprise and thoroughness. Developed by Germany, it was first used in the invasion of Poland.

Blitz "Lightning" – the name coined to describe the German bombing offensive against Britain in 1940-41.

Chancellor The German equivalent of prime minister.

Colony A country which is part of an Empire and ruled by the mother country: for example during the Second World War, India and other members of the British Empire apart from Dominions such as Canada, Australia and New Zealand, which were self-governing.

Communism A belief in a society that exists without different social classes and in which everyone is equal, and all property is owned by the people.

Concentration camp A camp where Nazi political opponents were imprisoned. During the war, *Untermenschen* and Jews were also sent there. Some camps, such as Treblinka and Auschwitz, were notorious "death camps".

Convoy A group of merchant ships sailing together with a warship escort.

Destroyer A fast, armed surface ship, smaller than cruisers and battleships and designed to protect them.

Fascism A far-right political system which depends on a strong dictator and repression of political opposition.

Holocaust The name applied to the "Final Solution" by which Hitler aimed to wipe out the Jewish people.

Intelligence The art of finding out the enemy's intentions. It involves gathering evidence through means such as spies and codebreaking, and interpreting that evidence.

Landing craft A ship designed to carry and land troops during a seaborne invasion.

Marines Soldiers attached to a navy whose primary role is to protect naval installations though they are often used for wider purposes.

National Socialist (Nazi) Party The political party founded by Hitler that assumed total power in Germany in 1934. It was dedicated to stamping out all opposition, expanding boundaries and asserting the primacy of an Aryan master race.

Partisans Armed resistance groups operating behind enemy lines. The term usually refers to resistance groups in Russia and Eastern Europe, notably Yugoslavia.

Propaganda The deliberate spreading of information (or misinformation) designed to further a particular point of view. Dr Goebbels was in charge of Nazi propaganda.

Rationing The sharing out of scarce resources so that everyone gets a fair share. In Britain, food, clothes and fuel were rationed during and after the Second World War.

Red Army The army of the Soviet Union during and after the Second World War.

Resistance Armed groups in an occupied country dedicated to the overthrowing of an invader.

Shell, shelling A shell is a large bullet fired by the big guns of the artillery. Shelling is the act of firing them.

Third Reich The new German Empire declared by Hitler on assuming dictatorial powers in 1934. The First Reich was the Holy Roman Empire under the Emperor Charlemagne in the ninth century. The Second Reich was the union of German states brought about by Count Otto von Bismarck after the Franco-Prussian War of 1871.

Treaty A binding agreement between nations. The First World War was ended by the Treaty of Versailles.

Torpedo An underwater missile fired from a ship or aeroplane. Torpedoes were the main weapon of German U-boats and caused huge Allied losses.

U-boat A German submarine. "U" stands for *untersee* (undersea).

INDEX

A

Afrika Korps 21, 28
aircraft carriers 16, 17, 21, 26, 27, 46
air raid 9, 12, 13, 23, 26, 32, 33, 36, 37, 43, 46
Allies 4, 5, 7, 9, 11, 14, 17-20, 22-29, 32, 33, 35-40, 42, 44, 46, 47
atomic bomb 23, 43-45
Australia 9, 17, 22, 23, 28, 46
Austria 8, 29
Axis powers 4, 5, 23, 29, 44, 46

B

Battle of the Atlantic 4, 18-19
Battle of Britain 12-13
Battle of Midway 26
Battle of the Bulge 38, 39
Blitz 12-13, 22, 32, 37, 46
Britain 4, 6-12, 16-26, 28, 32-34, 37, 41, 43, 44, 46, 47
British army 10, 11, 12, 20, 21, 28, 31, 36, 37, 39, 47

C

Canada 9, 19, 22, 36-38, 46
Chamberlain, Neville 8, 9
China 4, 16, 26, 46
Churchill, Winston 9, 10, 12, 13, 17, 20, 28, 36, 41, 44, 45
code-breaking 25
Cold War 45
concentration camp 24, 34-35

D

D-Day 25, 29, 33, 36-37, 42
Denmark 9, 23, 41
Dunkirk 11

F

First World War 6, 10, 18, 29
France 4, 6, 8, 9, 12, 16, 18, 20, 22, 25, 29, 36, 38, 39, 44, 46
invasion of 10-11

G

Germany 4, 6-12, 18, 20-23, 25, 29, 32-34, 36, 39, 41, 43, 44, 45, 46, 47

German air force (Luftwaffe) 10, 11, 12-13, 21
German army (Wehrmacht) 6, 8, 10, 11, 14, 15, 30, 31, 38, 40, 41
Greece 20, 21
Guadalcanal 26-27

H

Hiroshima 43, 44
Hitler, Adolf 4, 6, 7, 8, 9, 10, 11, 12, 13, 14, 15, 17, 23, 24, 31, 32, 34, 36, 39, 40, 41, 46, 47
home front 22-23
Holocaust 34-35, 45, 47

I

Italy 4, 7, 14, 20, 21, 23, 29, 31, 41
Iwo Jima 42

J

Japan 4, 16-17, 20, 23-27, 42-45
Japanese airforce 16-17, 23
Jews 14, 24, 34-35, 45, 46, 47

L

League of Nations 6, 44
London 9, 12, 13, 21, 37, 41

M

MacArthur, Douglas 17, 26, 42
Maquis 11, 22
merchant shipping 18, 19, 46
Montgomery, General 28, 38, 41
Mussolini, Benito 4, 7, 20, 23, 29, 41, 46

N

National Socialist (Nazi) Party 6-8, 11, 23, 35, 36, 44-47
New Zealand 9, 17, 23, 28, 46
North Africa 20-21, 28-29, 31, 36
Norway 9, 23, 41

O

Okinawa 42
Operation Barbarossa 14-15, 32
Operation Citadel 31

Operation Fortitude 36
Operation Overlord see also D-Day 36-37
Operation Sealion 12

P

Pearl Harbor 16-17, 20, 26
Poland 8, 14, 25, 34, 35, 38, 46
POW (prisoner of war) 24

R

radar 12, 13, 33
RAF (Royal Air Force) 11-13, 20, 21, 25, 32, 33, 37
rationing 22, 23, 47
resistance movements 11, 15, 22, 23, 25, 36, 38, 47
Rommel, Erwin 21, 28, 29, 36
Roosevelt, Franklin D 17, 26, 36, 40, 44
Royal Navy 18-21
Russia 4, 7, 8, 12-15, 23, 26, 29-32, 38, 43, 45, 47
Russian (Red) army 14, 15, 30, 31, 40, 43, 47

S

Secret Service 25
Stalin, Joseph 8, 14, 15, 30, 31, 44
Stalingrad 30-31

T

tank warfare 10, 14, 15, 22, 28, 31, 36, 38, 39, 40
Treaty of Versailles 6, 8, 44, 47

U

U-boat 18, 19, 25, 47
United Nations 44
USA 4, 6, 7, 13, 16, 17, 19, 22, 26, 31, 36-39, 41, 43-46
US airforce 32, 33, 43
US army 17, 26-28, 31, 36, 38, 39, 42
US Navy 16-17, 26, 27
USSR see Russia

V

VE Day 41